The Bus Driver's Threnody

for Sharon,
who lights my highway

Contents

Acknowledgements

City Arts (Tacoma): "Department of Storms . . ."

Floating Bridge Review #5: "The White Bus"

The Hopkins Review: "The Bus Driver's Threnody"; "The Driver Contemplates His Choice"; "Wants"

The Hudson Review: "A Benediction for the Bus"; "Emissaries of the Sunless Hours"; "Lost on the Bus"; "The Night Driver Shifts to Days"

Jack Straw Writers Anthology 2008: "Just a Vessel"

Measure: "The Pumpkin Tower"

The New Criterion: "Home for the Holidays"; "Thrown"

The New York Quarterly: "The Last Stop in Golden Gardens"

The North American Review: "Alien in Allentown"; "And Don't Forget the Fruit"; "Consensus"

The Sewanee Review: "The Night Driver" (vol. 118, no. 2, Spring 2010)

The Sewanee Theological Review: "Intersection"

The Southern Review: "The Night Driver Reads *The Night Driver* by John Cork"; "Perfect Attendance"

Southwest Review: "Riders in the Dark"

Tar River Poetry: "The Free Zone"; "Interstate"

"Alien in Allentown" and "Interstate" were reprinted in *Limbs of the Pine, Peaks of the Range* (Rose Alley Press, 2007)

"The Free Zone" was reprinted in *Tar River Poetry*'s Thirtieth Anniversary Issue (Fall 2008).

"Home for the Holidays" was featured on the *Poetry Daily* website on December 20, 2009.

"The Bus Driver's Threnody," "Home for the Holidays," and "Perfect Attendance" were reprinted in *Many Trails to the Summit* (Rose Alley Press, 2010).

"And Don't Forget the Fruit" and "The Bus Driver's Threnody" were reprinted in *New Poets of the American West* (Many Rivers Press, 2010); "The Bus Driver's Threnody" was selected for an Editor's Choice Award.

"The Last Stop in Golden Gardens" was reprinted in *Floating Bridge Review #4* (2011).

"Intersection" and "Wants" were reprinted in *Floating Bridge Review #6* (2013).

*

I wish to thank my fellow members of the Decasyllables for their assistance in helping me revise these poems: John Davis, Sharon Hashimoto, Susan Landgraf, Judy Lightfoot, Robert McNamara, Arlene Naganawa, Ann Spiers, and John Willson.

I also wish to especially thank Jim Barnes for his kind and continuous support of my work for the past four decades. Of those who have encouraged me, he has done so without stint since my days in the navy. My full gratitude to him, I cannot express.

Training Wheels

Take the wheel, the instructor sharply said
To the guy beside me. Aboard the oldest bus
In the yard—corners rounded off as if sanded,
Gray and red like a knife with a dried-blood kiss—

Our batch of new trainees had been taken out
To Alki just past dawn. Driven here
To see if I could steer a forty-foot
Metal bread box full of people, I was sure

This would be an easy job. How hard
Could it be? I had driven a grain truck
One summer, hauling peas in Tekoa. I ignored
The bat wings starting to flap in my stomach,

Tried to absorb the ease of the guy who held
The wheel with loose assurance—as though his hands
Gentled the bus like a horse. The trainer called
My name through my daydream. I set my behind

In the seat that felt soft as a sheet of plastic
Stretched over an anvil. I wanted work
Manual as the steering and the brakes,
The kind of job that wouldn't drown the spark

In my mind I needed to write. *Pull out
And head for the waterfront*, the instructor nodded;

Make sure to check your mirrors. I gripped
The slick black circle, leaned toward the road

And heaved, muscling the tires as I pressed
The gas. Like twisting the wheel on the steel door
Of a bank vault that wanted to stay shut.
We shuddered ahead. *Turn right at the corner*

And don't clip that telephone pole.
The slower I went, the heavier the bus grew;
The cracked blacktop grabbed at the wheels
As though the road was mud. I had to throw

My weight into steering. The right rear tire
Jumped the broken curb, jolting the coach
Like a spooked bronco. *Smoooooth*, the instructor
Drawled, frowning. *What did I tell you to watch?*

You gotta get this whole goddamn machine
To follow you around the turn. He rapped
A window with his knuckles. *Try again—*
And better. A squadron of bats now whipped

My innards to a squall with their wing tips.
Hunching over the wheel, I slowly slunk
To the main beach road and pulled to a stop.
I looked both ways: no one near us. I cranked

Firmly, gaze on the fish-eye mirrors, rounding
The corner without a bump. Someone said *Whew!*
I let my speed grow with my smile. *Hang*
A right at the next block; let's see you do

Two in a row. That's when the cartwheeling bats
Blew away what I'd heard in class: Pick
Your foot up first to brake. I tried to pivot
On my heel from the gas pedal, carried back

To how I drove my car, bearing down
On what I thought were the brakes while I hauled
Hard on the wheel, the bus like a runaway stallion
Galloping through the curve as the trainer yelled:

Stop, Stop, STOP! as we crossed the yellow lines
And I found the right pedal and bucked to a halt
A yard shy of a hydrant. I saw the veteran
In the bus parked nearby (before guilt

Could divert my eyes) laugh so hard, he bowed
To the steering wheel he pounded. The trainer set
His jaw like a parking brake: *If you're this bad*
This afternoon, I'm going to have to cut

You from the class. In Tekoa, told to fill
The water trough for the farmer's cattle, I'd forgotten
To turn off the hose. I hadn't thought I could feel
That same burning. The lunch I tried to eat

Scratched its way down my throat like a last meal.
Maybe I should've stay in the navy. But the gears
Of the day shifted: our final vehicle—
Gleaming white and gold as a dream of the future—

Had automatic brakes and steering. To fix
A turn going wide or short took a spin

Easy as a roulette wheel's. No creaks
From this bus—slowing didn't turn it to stone,

And its mirrors didn't come from some fun house.
Though the trainer watched me closer than I watched them,
I dodged his blade and made it through. *Guess
I'll have to let you stay,* he said. *A shame*

*About these new coaches: now anyone
Can drive a bus.* I still hear his voice
Sometimes, after all my years have run
Out on roads—when you work the brakes, they hiss.

Driving a Bus in Winter

An angry wasp, the alarm
Electrifies the sleep
Out of me. I suit up
And twist a key till my car
Growls awake. At the base—
A moment of light and dry—
I scrawl my name on the worksheet,
Then back outside. Rain
Crackles my jacket. Hunting
The rows of buses that hunch
Together like beasts in the cold,
I climb into mine. I press
A button, and the engine
Buzzes sharply: another
Mad insect. The heater
Whirs as I drive past the gate,
The tires hissing. By ones
And twos, I pull the people
Out of the dark. The bus
Fills slowly as the sky
Growing from black to gray—
As though the day comes
Simply because we all
Believe it will. The road
Unreels: a black tape
Measuring our journey.
We reach the edge of town
The same time as dawn.

Alien in Allentown

When Mister Mold climbs on my bus, he smells
Closed in: moist yet dusty—a dry well.

My nose wrinkles as I watch him grope
His sagging pockets. *Must be allergic to soap,*

I think. His coat is dark green like the clumps
Of moss making the roof of his shack slump

As if, lately, time has gained more weight.
I always see him shut his tilted gate

Carefully, tugging to be sure it's latched.
But what's to steal in Allentown? His hand—scratched

Deep across the knuckles as though from battle—
Narrows his coins to a trickle. They rattle

Individually down the metal throat
Of the fare box. The concentration he devotes

To their descent: Mister Mold might make
A wish. His lips don't move. When he takes

A seat, people near him change theirs.
They sniff and cough, though he seems unaware

Of their scorn as the bus curves along this road
They all live on, the leaf-brown river eroding

Its banks. But tonight, instead of gazing out
At shadowed hemlocks till the end of the route,

He suddenly gets up and switches seats.
The other riders then arise to retreat

To different spots, maintaining equal distance
From him as before. With a couple of grunts,

He's up again, plopping down this time
By the rear exit. The others grumble, climb

To their feet once more. I blink as I realize:
He's doing this on purpose. He catches my eyes

In the rearview mirror. While I grin back,
His wink is slow like moss growing over rock.

It Started Out with Edgar Allan Poe

One afternoon, riding my bus home
From keeping the books at the CPA's,
I heard, *It's Halloween.* Glancing up
From the business section (the SEC
Was looking into more accounting scandals),

Surprised the driver would announce such a thing,
I saw how dark it was outside. *Once
Upon a midnight dreary*, his mike intoned. . . .
The words began to register like a tune
I recognized but couldn't name. He got as far

As *the silken, sad uncertain rustling
Of each purple curtain* then paused: *That's all
I remember.* A man in the back started clapping;
A girl and her boyfriend by the rear door
Joined in. When these three people climbed aboard

Next evening, they sat up front. *Let's hear
Another*, I heard the girl say. I looked up
From the paper (Congress was vowing to block
The SEC) in time to see the three
Lean closer as though to hear better. The driver

Wasn't on his mike so I had to listen hard.
He *hmm'd* then did a short one. When he finished,
The boyfriend nodded, *"El Dorado"—cool.*

You know this one? He chanted, *Because I could*
Not stop for death and apparently reached the end,

Since the man said, *Good one. I used to know*
"The Tyger" by Blake—An older woman near him
With a simple *You mean?* launched right in.
When she was through, the two nodded, laughing.
The girl pointed at the man, *You*

And me, we gotta each do one tomorrow.
I peered through my reflection on the window
Into autumn. This time of year, you leave
In the dark and come home in the dark. It seems
The sun goes down as soon as it can.

They'd sit together, most days after that—
They called themselves the Up-Front Gang.
A seat at a time, I moved closer. What more
Did these people know? Sometimes a face
Would leave, a new one join: like numbers moving

Between the debit and the credit columns.
Like lungs contract and swell. I wanted to be part
Of all that breathing. Among my college texts
On risk assessment I found *An Introduction*
To Poetry. I thought I'd tossed that one out.

It had a line that made me smile. As I left
The bus next day, I faced the gang and bowed:
I will arise and go now. They laughed.
Bravo, the man clapped, then said to the driver,
It's all your fault—you and that damn bird.

The Nine-Pocket Macarena

Onto the Pacific Highway local bus he steps, then stops
When he sees the fare box: *Please pay*
As you enter. This seems a riddle he might solve with severe
    squinting.
He swats his legs for change—the sound
Of no coins clinking their little tinkly music makes him swat
    some more.
His frown deepens like a trumpet player's
Blowing and going for a note that won't be reached. Now his feet
Take up the beat: shifting foot
To foot like a sliver's in each one, he smacks the back pockets of
    his jeans, then waves
His hands around his jacket, outside
Inside, against his shirt, frisking himself for the crime of being
    dimeless.
His nose wrinkles as though he smells
An unseen fire scorching him, he's slapping so hard to put it out,
A powdered bitterness like ash
The taste in his mouth, he's about to flame up with shame when
    the driver
Truncates his routine: *Just sit down.*

Wants

The rider wants my name
And ID number. He claims

The bus I'm driving left him yesterday
Like a castaway

Abandoned on some uncharted atoll.
I've failed in my role

As captain of my vessel, he wants me
To know, and hopes that makes me happy.

Calmly I tell him I had the day off.
Expelling a laugh

Bereft of humor, his face is a sheen
Of vindication, eyes green

As antifreeze.
He wants me to please

Not add lying to the list
Of complaints he's calling in. He insists

On having my name. And I want
Right now to give it to him—and all the taunts

And griping that sitting here
Brings my uncloseable ears.

Instead, I keep my tone sober
When I say, *Ron Tober,*

ID Six Hundred
Sixty-Six. Armed with the name of the head

Of the bus company (retired
Years ago), the rider is now fired

Up to get me fired. Ignited
By the satanic light

I've sparked, maybe he thinks I've gone servile,
But at last I make him smile.

The Free Zone

The man climbs on my bus at Battery
And mutters, *Cops're always hasslin' me.*

I watch him in the rearview mirror, the smell
Of sweat and wine trailing him down the aisle—

The shoulder of his overcoat is torn,
A knit cap choking shaggy hair. When he turns

To sit by the back door, I see his face
Flushed as if from sun. But in this place,

A city on the edge of water, the rain
Falling for months has kept our eyes on the ground.

The man talks loudly to himself as I steer
The bus into traffic. Two teenagers

Sneer, then look away when he swings around.
He goes on talking: the sphere of his sound

Seals us in silence. A pretty girl across
From me stares back at him and whispers, "Gross."

He starts waving his arms, and I wonder if
He'll start a fight. Maybe he'll get off

Before we reach the end of the free zone—
The center of the city where no one

Has to pay. As I pull into the stop
At Yesler, the man suddenly jumps up

And yells, *No one better fuck with me!*
I unbuckle my seat belt when I see

Him glaring at the teenagers—they sit
As though caught in a cold wind. He spits

At them. I grab the radio phone
To call the cops: he's out the door and gone.

We breathe again; the brittle air breaks
With sighs and laughter. One teenager shakes

His fist, announcing, "Next time I'll kick his ass."
Some people near him cheer. "Maybe he's homeless,"

The girl says, smoothing her hair with a hand.
"Poor guy," she adds—as we leave the man behind.

Blood Tie

I'm twenty, but my mother goes with me
Each morning to the bus stop—*Because it's dark.*
She says she worries that something might happen
To a young woman like me—*You never know
What kind of crazy people ride the bus.*

So through the rain and cold, for half a mile
Mother strides beside me, her arm hooked
Around my waist. Under the streetlights, our shadow
Stretches and distorts like an amoeba
Moving on its pseudopods. In the bus shelter,

We take up the single seat. I feel the warmth
She means to give, her arm's weight on my shoulders
Like a mantle as Mom tells me to make sure
I have my fare, don't talk to strangers,
Have fun at work. I say I do, I won't, I will.

A long box notched with light, the bus
Finally pulls up and stops with a hiss.
Its doors open to pour out brightness
That makes my mother wince. No matter how fast
I get to my feet, she's right up with me.

Her embrace tightens as if to press her flesh
Into mine. Like every morning, she repeats
Take care, I love you, think happy thoughts.
Quickly I climb aboard. Does the driver hear
When I mutter through my frigid grin, *Shut up.*

Interstate

Zagging between the semis, cars, and vans
Without a turn signal, he switches lanes
The second he's entered one as if to throw
A demon off his scent. But who could follow
His swerving 4 x 4? What does he flee?
He drives as if distance were the enemy,
His wake a swirling cloak of blue-gray smoke:
The ghost of where he used to be. Rock
Blasts from his cab as though a band he's kidnapped
Is wailing for release. The drivers trapped
By speed and other limits—they're only slaves.
To part this sea of obstacles, he waves
The wand of his longest finger, conjuring
Their anger: the elixir that makes him young.

Jake on Wheels

I got a lot of bills to pay.
That's why I work so much O.T.
But I'd drive these buses anyway—
This job means everything to me.

That's why I work so much O.T.
My wife said, *Jake, we've hit the skids.*
This job means everything to me.
The judge gave her the house and kids.

My wife said, *Jake, we've hit the skids.*
I bought this camper off a buddy.
The judge gave her the house and kids.
It's dinged and cramped, but not too cruddy.

I bought this camper off a buddy.
It's parked in the employees' lot.
It's dinged and cramped, but not too cruddy.
If work needs me, I fill the slot.

It's parked in the employees' lot—
The one place where I won't get towed.
If work needs me, I fill the slot.
My favorite place is on the road,

The one place where I won't get towed.
On Papa's farm I learned to drive.

My favorite place is on the road.
Holding a wheel, I feel alive.

On Papa's farm I learned to drive.
I love to steer these big machines.
Holding a wheel, I feel alive.
The color for *dough* and *go* is green.

I love to steer these big machines.
I get folks where they want to go.
The color for *dough* and *go* is green.
This work ain't rocket science. So?

I get folks where they want to go.
She said, *Your job has zero class.*
This work ain't rocket science. So?
To change the view I hit the gas.

She said, *Your job has zero class.*
She said, *You never see the kids.*
To change the view I hit the gas.
You gotta move even if you skid.

She said, *Your never see the kids.*
I'll make it up when I retire.
You gotta move even if you skid.
The price of everything goes higher.

I'll make it up when I retire.
But I'd drive these buses anyway.
The price of everything goes higher.
I got a lot of bills to pay.

Wheels within Wheels

Ironic, isn't it? I joke as I'm brought
Onto the bus, *When I'm on board, that's wheels*
Within wheels! My humor goes for naught—
The driver's smile like grease slowly congeals.

So I tell him I don't need his help
Tying down my wheelchair; I grunt
With a laugh, *I've learned how to restrain myself.*
I've also learned to utter comments blunt

As these knobs of marble that pretend to be my knees.
My legs, dropping from them like concrete boots,
Are strapped together. *They might dance off without me,*
I say to the woman staring at them, a cute

Brunette who turns her face to the window.
People ought to be more polite. I scan
The seats behind me: sure enough, a row
Of scored and broken-down Ukrainians.

When the Iron Curtain fell to rust, the wind
From its collapse blew the ragged sails
Of their babushkas over here. I grinned
The first time I saw the luggage that trails

Them like pets—made from the hides of checkered beasts.
These food bank bandits stuff them full, go back

Home to unload, then out to snag another feast
At taxpayers' expense. I'm keeping track,

Though no one else is, in this welfare state.
We all should be treated equal when we reach these shores.
But now it's too late to close the gates—
What a sneaky way for them to win the Cold War.

When we reach my stop, I tell the driver, *Let
Me off first.* The Slavic hordes I feel
Bunching up behind me grumble. To set
My chair on the ground, I make the bus kneel.

The Pumpkin Tower

That day I wheeled my bus
Through a left–then–instant–
Right–hand turn, I saw
With amazement this place—
A domicile uprooted
From Burien or White Center,
The poorer end of this route.
The roof dark as needles
Of hemlocks, walls slightly
Lighter like lichen,
The small wooden house
Hunkered low as a mushroom
Among the columned edifici
Which lent the neighborhood
Of Magnolia (though the flower
Doesn't ever grow here
Naturally) the cachet
That only cliffs of cash
Confer. Its four conifers—
Growing close, ragged, thin
As mizzenmasts—poked
The sky like sticks in the eye
Of decorum, high above
The zoning laws. Bound
Together by a lattice
Of ladders and platforms, the trees
Became a tower. From the top

Of the tallest fir
A black flag flew:
A sort of Jolly Roger—
Its skull a pumpkin, crossbones
A pair of cornstalks.
The ensign for a ship
Of scarecrows? Did they hail
From the desiccated country
Of October? No man of straw
Could hoist such a sovereign pennant:
A Disunion Jack that snapped
With contempt at all the lawns
Scalped as though taking cues
From the felt of pool tables,
The dopey topiaries.
For this house sailed a green
Far from simple grass—
A roil of vines tangled
As snakes drowned the yard,
Leaves thrusting up
Like splashes made solid,
Splashes made by the pumpkins
Bobbing there—orange floats
Broken loose from a net
Gaudy and gigantic.
Climbing the tower's legs
Like Laocoön's, tendrils
Spiraled double helixes
Toward the dark flag
As if trying to realize

Its depicted apotheosis:
When a new dawn—its sun
Ribbed as a stout hull
And stuffed with seeds—will sail.

Myrtle Talks

Though that's my given name, I gave it away
One day way back in college. *Mert*
Is what I go by. Know what the Greeks say

About myrtle? I heard my professor blurt
This out in class—a crown of it decorated
The brows of those not worthy of laurel. That hurt.

It's thirty years since we were "liberated,"
Yet the dough the doe receives is still around half
The buck the buck is paid. *Mandated*

By the marketplace, claim the men who staff
The control panels of life. *But soon*, they croon. . . .
Till then I'll drive a bus. This makes them laugh,

But that Ralph Kramden crap is a cartoon:
These rigs have automatic brakes and steering.
(Did you ever see that loud-mouthed, fat buffoon

Drive?) On the road, no supervisor clings
Like that Wal-Mart manager when I was a "Sales
Associate." The only glass ceiling

Between me and the world is the windshield. "Female
Driver" is still a punch line for some guys
Who like to think they'd like to punch. My nails

Are scarlet razors. And if someone tries
To swing on me like Kramden threatened to sock
His wife, I'll go in a shot not for his eyes

But his face: that's where the nerves are. Some gawk
When they climb on—*How can a little gal
Like you do this job?* And lewd back talk

From drunks . . . or teenagers, those criminals-
In-training. Usually it's all just show.
The one you have to watch, you see his smile

Grow wider as his eyes narrow.
After this long, I'm onto most of the tricks.
Soon as I start to smell things going

Out of orbit, I call the cops right quick.
And when payday comes, in my jacket pocket—
Next to the tube of Mace—I stick my check.

The White Bus

He'd never seen a bus
Colored the *non* of frost.
Who ran this rival line?

Over its windshield,
The reader board shone blank
As though its destination

Bore no name. The sides
Were free of advertising,
Even logos. When waved at,

The other driver nodded,
Uniform maroon
As blood long mixed with earth.

The length of darkened windows
Looked wrong—almost opaque—
As if the bus carried

Something burning. Limousines
Had tinted glass; therefore
Its riders must be special.

Between the setting sun
And him, the bus passed—
The glare through its windows

Briefly engraved a row
Of heads like charred stumps.
He saw in his rearview

The white bus turn
Onto a side road—the one
That led to the state prison.

Twin Lakes in the Fog

The maple leaves have gone, though rusty ghosts
Pressed into the concrete of the sidewalk
Mark where they rested longest, before the wind

Made off with them again. Tonight, a mist
Seems to draw the empty bus shelters back
Into uncertain haze. Its voice is the sound

Of a frog: a bottle's cork that someone twists
Now and then. Blurred as Twin Lakes,
The heads of shredded cattails try to bind

Their tatters with this white air. Encased
In vapor, the bare maples become black
Webs holding the fog. Their dark strands

Slowly gather the gray until a coyote
Is released to watch all shelter fade.

Department of Storms: From Inside the Bus, the Bartender Sees a Sign

To be in charge of lightning, shimmying veils
Of rain, wind that backhands the hemlocks down—
That's the job she wants.

                  Think of the fear
She could inspire, sharper than the kind
That makes her cringe when she sees police or soldiers,
Anyone in uniform.

                  She would make
Her *own* uniform: gray as basalt, contours
Darker than thunderheads, and gloves
With fingertips a searing white.

                  Assigning ice
To overpasses, hail the size of grapeshot
To star the windshields of SUVs
Oblivious till now,

                  she would overthrow
Power lines and cell phone towers,
Unleashing torrents to blow away the sun,
The carapace of its light.

Asphalt

I bought a 4 x 4, you say,
Hooking your thumbs in your belt loops.
Your father laughs and turns away.
Because you're dumb as a post? he whoops;

*Tell me what you're going to haul
Besides your worthless ass.* The urge
To hit him—you feel your fists ball.
Instead, when you leave, a surge

Of power to your huge tires
Rattles a rooster tail
Of rocks against his house. The roar
From your engine swamps his wails;

Your rearview shrinks him like a slug
Dropped in a pool of brine. *They'll pay
Attention now*, you shout; *I'll drag
The whole goddamn freeway!*

Screaming up I-5, you whip
Around the vans and RVs,
Their horns your chorus as you flip
Them off. Then you zag left to squeeze

Between two semis—and climb
The beveled concrete barrier
Dividing come from go. In no time
Airborne, you hear your laughter

Changing pitch the way your tires
Suddenly whine higher: they spin
Fast enough now to fire
A new road, and the sky lets you in.

Perfect Attendance

The hurdles to work that hamper the rest of us
Never keep Vernon Burke from driving his bus.

Despite the roads iced like cod in the hold
Of a trawler, fish-tailing trucks that rolled

And blocked his exit, he still sails in. Clock
That fails to be alarmed when a storm knocks

The power out? Vern has a backup windup.
The beater's starter stutters to a stop?

Vern takes the spare pickup. Even with fevers
And colds these thirty years, he's a believer

In always showing up. This morning he crawls
In with flu—*my riders' gift*, he sniffs. *I'd call*

In sick, I say. With a sound like gargling phlegm,
Vern laughs: *I gotta give it back to them.*

The Driver Contemplates His Choice

What stupid calculus
Told him driving a bus
Would be the way to reach
A writer's life? To teach
Would be hours marking papers
By surly teenagers
Who only saw their degrees
As passports to the countries
Of wealth and status. Math
Had been his major: a path
Certain to bring success
Of the kind that counted. Useless,
Though, to someone stirred
Unexpectedly by words.
After serving a tour
In the navy, he washed up
Once more on shore, then dropped
Into a life he never
Foresaw at all—a clever
Variation on "the command
Of a vessel" which his own hand
Steers. But it hauls a mob
He can't court-martial: the job
At first he tolerates,
He slowly grows to hate.
It pays really well
For dumb labor, he tells

Himself, *and I don't race*
Home with a briefcase
Of papers I need to grade.
Instead, his nerves are frayed
By traffic, drunks, and kids
He longs to get rid
Of as soon as they board.
He remembers (between hordes)
He'd planned to use his time
Off to follow rhyme
And rhythm into places
A bus can't go. When he faces
A blank page, he finds
Only numbers entwined
Like fiery afterimages
Burn its expanse: addresses
He's told to watch out
For, the numbers of his routes,
Timepoints he must make,
The petty fares he takes.
He puts his pen away
For good. The next day,
When he reaches for a transfer,
It paper-cuts his finger.

Lost on the Bus

Umbrellas lie folded up
Like bats asleep.

The drunk, crumpled
As his sack of Mad Dog, is dumped

On the back seat by the cops. Black knit caps
Are left behind: some who worship

The night have renounced their faith. Temple pressed
Against the glass, the woman rides all day and twists

Her transfer till she wrings its time
To nothing. Nickels and dimes

Are stuck like random offerings in the cracks of seats
To buy safe passage. In his camo jacket,

Ears wired, the teenager fills
A head so full of music, he must wail.

Just a Vessel

I see the driver reading as I board
His parked bus. *You want something* really *good?*
I ask, forcing a smile. *Just try the Lord
And His Book. The Holy Bible has withstood*

The test of time—it's the best best seller!
I unzip the leather cover: sun glistens
On its gold-edged pages. *Too zealous,*
I think of myself; the driver barely listens

And says like a banker refusing me a loan,
No thanks—I'm agnostic. Sitting down,
I try, *God believes in you.* The words drown
In the noise of his engine starting. My tailbone

Begins to hurt from my stiff posture—I hate
To proselytize. Does God truly exult
In them who spread His Joy? *To pass the gates
Of heaven,* I offer weakly, *the wise consult*

*The Book and find the truth of God's Word.
Doubt is something all of us must wrestle.*
He grunts, *Distracting me's a safety hazard.*
Slumping, I mutter, *I am just a vessel*

Of the Lord. I feel tired. When did the well
Of my faith begin to dry up? I'm torn

By the selfish need to see a sign. *Hell!*
The driver yells, slamming the brakes, his horn

Blaring at a pickup heading straight
For the side of the bus. I sit up: there's no one
Behind the wheel! I can see it's too late
For us to dodge it, so I just hold on.

The truck slams *whump!* Cursing, the driver parks;
We climb out to look. This moment frees us
From our routines. As he rubs at the dent marks,
I see painted on the tailgate *Jesus.*

Intersection

The roads have grown religious. Crosses sprout
By narrow streets as bent as paper clips.
They line the off-ramps exiting from doubt.
Along the edge of last, unscheduled trips,
Bouquets blunt corners where faith collides
With physics. Names are fixed to photographs
Of faces when time still let them smile. Beside
The sticks, candles gutter. Guardrails buckled in half
Mimic the altar of a church whose walls
Are absent. Like a choir sparse and ragged, crows
That pick at bits of shattered glass squall
As if declaring some borders open as others close.
And death, with these tilted-X displays,
Becomes a surveyor staking out its causeways.

The Last Stop
in Golden Gardens

As I reach it, I park the bus.
On my left a vacant lot
Too shallow to hold a house
Let me look for years
Out across the bay
To the Olympics. They rasp
The sky with their jagged line.
But the peaks that matter
In this age are those on graphs,
Marking the altitudes of money.
A blueprint saw the land
Wasn't big enough: more
Was trucked in. Like a forest
Made square, two stories
Of beams and rafters rise—
As if the final end of want
Is to make beauty private.
I want to hate the workers,
But they're just young men:
When they see me watching,
They wave. They're nailing
And planing the walls of a box—
A camera that over and over
Will take the same picture,
Its owner keeping his view
By staying in the dark. Starting
The engine, I wave goodbye.

A Benediction for the Bus

Unexpectedly a day will come that dumbs
Complaints of deadbeat seniors, unwashed bums,
And teenagers who—trying to prove they're grown—
Curse like the parents they hate. The ring tone
Springing suddenly into the stagnant air
Won't tear the driver's ear like razor wire.
The *thrum* he feels through the gas pedal becomes
A joyful quivering from the road; tires skim
The blacktop current of this riverbed.
He'll smile while the traffic lights withhold their red
And let the green of Douglas firs and maples
Wave his bus on its course, branches full
Of wind to caress and let go. The wheel will slip
Through his fingers smooth as water in his grip.

Consensus

To drive at night can be lonely—behind the wheel
Is the darkest place on the bus. I feel cut off
From the passengers lit dimly in their seats.
As I'm going past a stop, the bell rings.
I keep driving. A big kid comes up: *You missed
My stop.* Eyes on the road, I say he rang
Too late to stop safely. He growls, *Fuck you.*

The next stop is several blocks away.
I'm wondering what to do, when an old man
In the aisle seat directly across from me
Pipes up. *He's right, pal; you pulled too late.*
The punk turns to face him. *The shit I did,*
He spits. The other says louder, *You waited
Too long to ring. Too slow means no go.*

Fuck you, repeats the kid. The only riders
Besides this pair are sitting in the center
Of the bus—three longshoremen coming home
From swing shift. The grimiest of them says,
Zip it, dickhead—you shoulda rung before.
As the punk looks around, the old man laughs:
So fuck you! The kid's head swings back—

Fuck you! he replies. All the longshoremen
Like a Greek chorus yell, *FUCK YOU!*
As though it's a stage direction, I pull the bus
Into the next stop. The doors hiss open;

45

The kid looks my way. *I know*, I say—
Fuck me. Diving out the door, he flips
Off everyone. We all laugh like family.

Shake-Up
(when bus drivers are allowed
to change their work schedules)

That goddamn Karl should just retire,
Grumbles Jeff, a fellow driver.
The bastard's been here forty years!

Jeff stares at the board and pokes
The list. *Why the hell does he take*
Something different each day of the week?

He's gotta know that only traps
The rest of us into splitting up
Our own assignments. Loada crap—

Must do it just to piss us off!
Then Frank lets loose his dry laugh:
I been workin' here long enough

To know. Karl used to always pick
The same run. He got to like
The riders; you know the way he jokes.

But then one day this guy pulls out
A combat knife. Says he'll cut
Karl's throat if he don't keep quiet.

Frank shifts his weight a bit and blinks.
Cops later tell Karl he's got spunk,
Keepin' his cool. "I just went blank,"

Karl says to me after—"Couldn't talk
For a couple days." Jeff shakes
His head: *The guy must* really *be sick*

To still stay with this job. Frank smiles,
Not him; his wife. Needs the medical.
So Karl is stuck here. Don't tell

Him I toldja this. Well, time to get
My bus and hit the road. We wait
A minute and follow Frank out.

The Development

Was this man. Lived in this "development."
What the realtor called it. Reminded him
Of that crack TV's Riley made: "*Whadda revoltin'*
Development DIS is!" Behind his house—
Looked just like the joints either side of his—
A fence. Eight-foot, planks of pine. Ran
All the way around his block. Blocked
His view of the Park 'n' Ride. But the buses:
Heard their diesel wheezing as they died
To stop there. Noise finally brought him out
Past that thin wood wall. Saw this strip
Of dirt between the sidewalk and fence—rocks,
Weeds, chunks of beer bottles. Thought:
Coulda stuck a couple trees here, goddamn
Builders. Decided right then. Grabbed a saw.
Cut through his covenant, made a gate
To let him out. *You can't*, neighbors nixed.
Said it more when he dug the dirt, cleared
The rocks, pushed seeds down in. *Not*
Your property, neighbors scowled. He shoved
A birch sapling, some rhododendrons
Into holes. Patted the dirt. Said, *Is now.*

Letter of Condolence

Dear Driver:
          We regret that you were punched
Unconscious by some troubled juveniles
Last Saturday past midnight. Kindly fill
Out the form attached. Since we have launched
A full review (and the press exaggerates
Events sometimes), the bus company needs you
To detail what you did or didn't do
That might have upset the minors. Though forced to cut
Security and raise the fares once more—
The recession hit us hard—we feel certain
These factors played no part in what was done.
Please get well soon. Focus on your future
Behind the wheel. Be assured the company needs
You back and wants to see you on the road.

What He Knows

He knows his friends are tired of hearing him gripe
About how tired he's grown of having to drive
The bus. He knows he could have ended up

Being a knocker, swinging a sledge to stave
In skulls of cows on the cattle drive to hamburger.
Or working some worse job. He'd like to prove

His dim view wrong, agree his riders *are*
Friendly, or at least not drunk or dangerous,
At least not most of them. They pay their fare,

Or at least most of it, at least most of them. Yes,
He knows—to quit would just be crazy: he owes
His car, his house, his bank account to the bus.

It's thirty years. Who else does he suppose
Would hire him now? This is what he knows.

The Bus Driver's Threnody

To be
    a fireman:
        his childhood wish
Lies drowned.
    He suffers
        from *almost-growns*
            who fish
For change
    they never carry;
        near-deaths who take
            so long
To find a seat
    (each one they pass
        is wrong
For their august
    buttocks);
        you're-lates
        who complain
About the gridlock,
    stupid drivers,
        the rain;
The *shouts*, dressed
    in prison chic,
        who strut-walk
To the back
    and sit down far
        apart
        to talk.

And *wanh-hanhs*:
        little
           liabilities
Whose parental
        pacifiers
           whine, "Please
Sit down—
      the bus might
          hit a bump!"
He moans.
     At least
        the garbage
           in a dump
Truck is still
     and quiet.
        Reaching the end
           of the route,
He imagines
    a huge hose
        blasting them out.

And Don't Forget the Fruit

Miss Fargnoli climbs the slick steps—the rain
Is light though steady. *Old Seattle plain,*
She tells me with a sigh: *little drops*
But lots of them. The first rider I stop
For and the last to leave, she always takes
The spot across from me. After she shakes
The water off her orange umbrella, she sits
Carefully in the Lonely Hearts' Seat—
The place where people park when they're full
Of need for a priest in this confessional
On wheels. Although small and seventy,
She doesn't lament an awful life. Like a key
Whose twist removes a set of ankle chains
From the slog of the hours, her comments train
My thoughts on the world beyond the windshield.
Worn as a Labrador, but well heeled,
She says, umbrella poking my gym bag
On the floor beside the fare box. The fabric sags
As though collapsed in sleep. *It's never bitten*
Anyone, I joke. Our conversation flits
To exercise—I tell her a life behind
The wheel can lead to a life that's *all* behind.
She waves a hand: *Some drivers, oh my Lord!*
I don't see how they can get aboard
Without the wheelchair lift. Now, me, I swim
A dozen laps a day—that keeps me trim.
The image of this tiny woman kicking
The water out of the Y pool brings

A smile to my lips. *Back when I had my car,*
She allows, *I learned how stupid people are.*
My bumper sticker declared, "I oppose
Adipose." When I laugh, she grins: *No one knows*
What that means these days. A man asked me
If I was against slouching. Dictionaries
Must now be foreign as the Rosetta Stone.
I tell her I watch what I eat, though I'm prone
To chocolate binges. *It always seems that sweets*
Are what lead one's diet to defeat.
Eat vegetables—and don't forget the fruit!
I still have all my teeth. She shows me, then hoots
At her display. I say I usually take
An apple, grapes, something to chew on my break
At the end of the line. *Along with the candy bars?*
She teases. The bell rings; I edge some cars
And stop at the curb. A man with a keg of a beer
Gut comes up and climbs off as soon as the door
Opens. I call out that he still owes his fare.
Turning around slowly, he gives me a stare,
Then slides a hand deep into his coat.
I feel a dryness tightening my throat
When he says, *Know what happened to the last bastard*
Who told me to pay? I cut 'im. Somehow I'm stirred
To lean and reach into my bag. *You know*
What happened to the last guy to show
Me a knife? I shot him. He licks his lips,
Taking a step away, and nearly trips
As he hurries off. When I lean back, I hold
A banana in my hand. A wave of cold

Goes through me, a grin frozen to my face.
Miss Fargnoli laughs as her umbrella traces
An arabesque in the air. *If he'd gone haywire
And come back on, I'd have punctured his spare tire.*

Turn in the Direction of the Skid

Ignore the prickling of your skin when the hide
Of snow the road has grown begins to slide

> The wheels out from under your tightening grip.
> The road is testing you. As your bus slips

Sideways toward the ditch that widens to swallow
Your driving career, fight the call to follow

> Your fears: steer away from the scheduled route
> For just a moment. Moves the sun taught you are moot

When the blacks of tire and asphalt can't meet.
To reach true north, the closer you get

> To the pole, the more you need to deviate
> From the way the compass arrow points. Straight

Emerges from a series of small curves
The road is throwing you. Lean into them and swerve.

Home for the Holidays

At four p.m. the day before Christmas,
There's no one on my bus.
Dark as midnight; everyone's bailed out.
I slow to a stop at the foot
Of the hill to Lakeridge. Snow
Beneath the street lamps glows
Slick as melted plastic. Two cars
Abandoned in the ditch endure
Their gradual erasure, flakes
Stippling out their color. I look
At the snow tapping the windshield
And call Control. Afraid I'll get stalled,
I ask if this road's been closed. *No—*
Continue on regular route. I swallow.
Can I get this big machine to the crest?
I lean forward and press the gas.
Halfway up
I begin to slip—
Snow chains scrabble like a planer
Over the ripples in a warped board.
The tires whine and skirr,
But the bus isn't moving. In a nearby yard
A girl staring makes me stop and set the brake.
No bigger than the snowman beside her, she kicks
Its stomach; like ghosts of winter, they gleam
In the light from my windows. The engine hums
When I climb out, as though it's wondering, *What now?*
Beats me—I should've been driving a plow.

Can you fix it? yells the girl. I trudge
Over, clouds of breath bringing my fridge
To mind, and the turkey stuffed inside it.
Hope so, I smile, but from her side of the street,
All I see is a bus that's stuck
As a lit-up block of ice. A snowball smacks
My arm; when I turn, the girl laughs and flings
Another. Then her eyes widen: *Your bus is leaving*
Without you. I whip around—it's starting to slide
Slowly backward. It's gaining speed
As I lurch-run toward it. When I reach
The middle of the road, all I can catch
Is the sight of the bastard receding like a flare
Dropped down a well. Missing the cars
And the ditch, my runaway steers true
As a toboggan in its chute.
Oh Lord, let it get all the way to the flat
And just hit
Some snowbank! But then it hooks a left, loudly cracks
Aside a wooden fence and—the angle blocks
My view. Hurtling down the slope, I snag
A mailbox, whacking my leg
Against what's left of that fence. The bus has punched
Through the front of a house: it looks clenched
In a ragged mouth. I knock on the door
That's been knocked in and call out—no one's here.
Squeezing through, I turn off the engine.
The house inside is dark as the den
Of some beast, so I find the kitchen light,
Call Control again. After a long quiet,
I hear, *You'll have to wait a while; there's lots*

Of buses tied up now. I figure I'll sit
Back in my seat, but a car pulls up
In the driveway. Sighing, I lick my lips
And go out to meet the owner. She whistles
When she sees the wreckage, then grimly smiles:
I didn't want to cook tonight anyway.
I'm apologizing for everything, but she says,
I need some hot chocolate. You want some?
I feel myself nod, my face numb.
Gathered in her kitchen, the three of us
Sit close as kin—this woman, me, and my bus.

Immigrants

I come from Pisky, north Ukraine: it's just
Outside Chernobyl's Zone of Alienation.
Contaminated by the ticking dust—
That's how they see us, some Americans.

I'm glad to be here in their land, but it's hard
To leave behind my own. Lucky I learned
English before; I help my friends get cards
To stay here. Riding the bus, we take turns

To get groceries. Our driver points his thumb,
Asks what's in our baggage that makes us stoop.
He laughs when I smile and say, *Plutonium.*

Our women wear scarves, our men wear coats too tight,
Threadbare; but our sneakers are glowing white.
We become American from the ground up.

A Rainbow in My Pocket

I love to ride the bus: I get off by getting on
And traveling around. I grin to have a grumbling vehicle,
Big as the single-wide I live in, cart my carcass

Everywhere—me, a guy. When I ascend the steps,
The driver asks to see my transfer. Furrowing my brow,
I make a show of checking pockets. I say I need to find it

And head back to take a seat. I smile at those around me
As though I have a rainbow in my pocket—this ensures
They'll look away. Then I take the rainbow out and thumb

My way through its bands of color, each arranged by alphabet.
I noticed when I climbed aboard that the transfer for today
Is a red R. I slide one loose from the stack I've saved

For years: somewhat smudged and tattered, but this will wave me
    through.
The wad goes back in my pocket. How much would I have had to
    pay
If someone had invented a slip of paper that dissolved

After a day? Just like a rainbow vanishing when clouds
Check the sun. I smile at all the riders—they gaze at anything
But me—and face the way that everyone is going.

Thrown

I've only started stabbing at the snow
That chokes my driveway when I hear the rumble
Of the pickup: it comes around the corner
From the hidden end of this dead-end street.

Its *wub-wub-wub-wub* seems a kind of mutter,
As if the truck is mulling over what risk
This road is paved with. Trying to ignore
The noise, I thrust at the frozen hide that crusts

My blacktop. No matter how hard I lunge,
This spade—made for turning earth in summer—
Bites only little moon-slices from the ice.
The truck rolls forward lazy as the flakes

Shivering down. BLAH DA-DA-DA! it bellows,
A wad of exhaust black as diesel hawked
At the cold, the notched edges of its tires
Blurring as they whine for grip. I hear the squeals

Of a boy, though the driver's alone in the cab.
When the truck zooms by, I see a kid on a sled
Tethered to the back bumper. His yells
Echo against my house as he just misses

My mailbox by maybe the length of a hand.
Snow sprays as his father spins the pickup
Into a cul-de-sac across from me,
The sled swinging like a pendulum.

I tell myself that I should do something:
Shout at the driver blinded by the blizzard
He swirls around himself; or call the cops.
The pickup slide-skids the arc of the circle,

The sled whipping across the buried borders
Of the neighbors' lawns. The rear tires steam
As if melting. The driver blasts his air horn,
And the wheels scream when he charges back

Toward the dead end. The sled is empty now,
Flipping on its line. A different shriek
From the cul-de-sac makes me turn:
The thrown boy is standing washed in blood.

Holding my shovel like a spear, I plunge
Across the street, fighting to keep my balance.
I'm nearly on top of the kid before I see
It's just a red snowsuit. He backs away,

Arms up to shield himself, and starts to bellow
For his father. *It's okay*, I tell him, but now he's crying,
And I hear the truck loom up behind, can feel
The hammering of the engine against my back.

What's going on? the man demands, jumping
Out of the pickup which he leaves running:
It trembles like a beast. *I thought he was hurt*, I say,
Afraid to lower my shovel. But I do.

For a while, the snow flutters through the steam
Of our breath—I watch flakes melt on the windshield.

The man grunts; his shoulders unhunch. He shifts
His glare from me to the boy. *C'mere!*

Circling me, the kid stops short of his father.
He staggers a bit when the man throws an arm
Roughly around him. *Can't stay on that sled,*
His father grumbles, giving him a shake,

I ain't takin' you out no more. The boy
Jerks his head up: *Daaad!* he begs, the word
Stretched out to a three-note cry
That dips in the middle like a power line

Sagging with snow. The man points; the kid
Climbs awkwardly into the cab.
Shooting me a look, the driver gets in.
I'm sure he'll gun the engine, but he backs out

Slowly, angling the pickup as though he thinks
The road is ice over a deep channel.
The truck recedes, the snow sanding it
To gray translucence till it fades from view.

Unsteadily, I walk through the shimmer.
The moon-bites in my driveway are gone.
I grip the shovel as I hear the ticking of snow
Like thousands of tiny teeth biting back.

Emissaries of the Sunless Hours

They board his bus near midnight. He knows
These three are trouble: leather jackets black
With rain and woven from the dark, the studs
Of metal glinting randomly as stars.

The one who comes on first is thin but tall,
Hair blue as lapis, face pale as the fangs
The driver's pretty sure are porcelain.
As sure as he is this trio will stiff him. Coins

Sliding like liquid from his fingers, the Goth
Looks at him: *May I please have a transfer, sir?*
The driver waits for something more smart-ass
As he hands him one. Bluehair nods, *Thank you.*

Polite as well, the other two follow him
To the bench seat in the back. *I won't go near
That seat*, an older woman told the driver
This evening—*that's where all the assholes sit.*

In the rearview he sees a guy in a ball cap
And Husky sweatshirt (the driver's alma mater)
Grin and shake his head as the three pass,
Saying something to a girl across the aisle.

She ignores him, the wire to her earbuds
Trembling like a bifurcating vine

In a breeze as her head shakes to a private tune.
The bus goes by another dozen stops

Before the bell rings. Ball Cap gets up,
Leaning down as if to talk to her again,
Then snatches at her iPod. She yelps, clinging
To the thing while he growls, *Gimme that, bitch!*

The driver's calling the cops when he hears and feels
A thud through his boot soles. The tall Goth
Has tackled Ball Cap in the aisle, his friends
Piling on, pinning him down. *Give it back!*

The thin one says as the other two twist
Ball Cap's arms behind him till he squeals.
Bluehair hands the device to the girl; her hand
Shakes as she takes it. *Now lemme up!* yells

The thief. *Soon as the cops arrive*, says the Goth,
Looking up at the driver. *Right, sir?*
The driver nods, grinning: *From now on, any time
You take my bus, you guys ride for free.*

Riders in the Dark

As if in honor of the night, they wear
All black and stand as motionless as mourners.

The bus stops are veiled behind the curtain
Of rain that glimmers and shreds like old nylon,

Behind the trees releasing people
Unexpectedly as dryads. The arrival

Of the bus gives shadows depth, lets them throw
Their shapes into this vessel they merely borrow.

In the unlit gaps where the stops lie, a stump
Can look like a passenger. The driver stomps

The brakes for the concrete post: light-colored pants
Is what he took it for. A shifting darkness haunts

The bus shelters—open mausoleums
Anything might enter. Longing to pass them,

He feels his thumb tap the wheel till he's clear.
He'd thought he was the only constant here,

The riders phantoms. But the endless dips and swells
In the road tell him the course he travels

Is a river—and all night long, he's nothing more
Than Charon, the soul who'll never step ashore.

The Night Driver
—Route Number Seven, One a.m.

A quiet autumn night. In the back a pair
Of drunks, the only riders, are passed out
Like casualties from some undeclared war.

Nearly hearing the slosh in their stomachs (vats
That want no stirring), I smell their bouquet:
Lilacs in sour milk. We ease to the light

At Forty-Third and University.
As if reglazing my windshield, the rain
Melts the beads of its broken rosaries.

The wipers hiss; I wait for the red to green.
A Toronado roars up on my left—tires
A sound of fabric tearing. The car runs

The light, swerving right around my bumper
To rock to a stop at the corner curb. A man
Leaps out and rushes over to pound my door.

Is Sheila on here? he yells. *Lemme on!*
He wears a tilted red felt hat, a crucifix
Mixed up with coils of silver chains

Looping his throat. I shake my head. He kicks
The door, his glare fiercer than the curses
Familiar to this route. The back of my neck

Prickles when the man attempts to force
The door open. Giving a scream, he's gone.
When did the light turn green? Its brightness pierces

The cataracts of ice my eyes had grown—
My foot floors the pedal. Too soon, I slow
For the last stop and park. I pry my hands

From the slick steering wheel. I've got to go
Back to that intersection. *He won't*
Be there, I whisper; the drunks snore away.

Boots rooted to the sidewalk, he rants
At a woman dressed too lightly for this weather,
His car double-parked in my lane. But some saint

Of mischief made him leave the driver's door
Open. At this hour, no one else is out.
A smile splits my face. Blasting the horn,

I stomp the gas. The man gargles a shout
That's lost in the slam and shriek of steel: a gust
Of glass like solid rain sequins his hat.

I'm calling the cops when he charges up, the mist
Outside blurring his face to a glow. The slice
Of my grin is a wound I want him to taste.

He threw that door wide just as the bus
Was going by, I tell the nodding cops;
Nothing I could do. The man's so mad, I could trace

The vein in his temple. He grabs his chains and snaps
The cross from his neck. When the cops make him sit
In their prowler, he sags. Some bits of glass slip

From his brim to the carpet, glinting at his feet.
The surge of rapture that swelled me when I hit
His door now leaves, and the rain stops just like that.

The wall of clouds that choked the sky retreats.
Inside the bus, I forget how much blackness
Is pressing down on all of us at night.

The Night Driver Reads
The Night Driver by John Cork

I've felt this fear:
I'm driving my bus through miles
Of condensed dark when a man appears

Dead ahead,
His scream my scream as his body
Thuds aside to the stench of brakes

Scorching, my foot
Slamming as if through the floor.
I feel I'm right there with the Driver

At the same time
I know I'm just reading
This graphic novel. When the Driver stops,

The body gets up
And grabs the door handle.
The almost victim doesn't seem hurt

When he asks the Driver
To take him to the hospital.
His eyes stare a deeper red

Than brake lights
As he rasps, *I haven't slept
For nine days*. I've felt transported

To another zone
While driving a bus long
Into the sunless distances—

Bodiless
From concentrating on the strip
Of black ahead. I'm sure I've carried

Riders like him:
His skin the thinnest sheath
Stretched over a rage that strains

For a target.
I've felt a strange tide
Rippling through my skin in the hours

Of deepest shadow
That no one sees but the Driver.
When borders blur, rage and fear

Can cross like a virus,
And behind the wheel I've thought
The words the Driver keeps repeating:

I'm only trying
To get home. Bodies
Begin to appear along the road

Like signposts.
A cop picks up the trail
And catches the Driver attacking his wife

With the same tools
Left in the Driver's car
By the man he hit. The Driver grins—

Eyes redder
Than the strobe on the cop's cruiser.
The same car that soon pulls over

A group of teens
Speeding through the night.
The cop who climbs from the prowl car

Is the Driver.
He tells the teens, *Step out
Of the vehicle and no one*

Will get hurt.
Now when my bus hits
Something—an unseen part of the dark—

I feel the fear
I'm running over all the lives
I might have lived instead of this.

The Night Driver Shifts to Days

He hates to wake up early, but he hates
To work late even more. So the clock rings
The sleep out of him, the blackness clinging
To his open eyes dull as a film of slate

His dreams won't transfer to. He used to drive
The graveyard shift, and that's what it had seemed—
In his bus, some eyes after sundown gleamed
Like those of the walking dead. Their stare gave

Him the feeling people weren't held as tight
In their skins: the way he'd slow for a stop light
Just enough to glance left and hang a right.
It's easier to turn on red at night.

He thought his skin had thickened over time,
Believing he'd grown used to the sort of sights
The dark could bring—the drunks, occasional fights
In the back, teenagers bragging about crimes

He guessed they might actually have done.
And driving at night meant fewer riders,
Lighter traffic, almost no supervisors
To catch him making a mistake.

                    Then that man
Waved the knife at him; jumped off and ran.

His friends tell him he hauls as many crazies
By day—they're just hidden in the crowd. He replies:
In the sun, they have to keep their faces on.

Aurora

—for Mark McLaughin, Driver #2106

I. The Driver

I've whistled lots of songs while driving a bus:
"Aqualung" by Jethro Tull for the guy
In the red sweatshirt who smells and has to touch
The floor; Madonna's "Like a Virgin"
For the girl whose purple hair and tight tank top
Reveal that she wants attention but who glares
With teenage scorn when someone looks at her;
"If I Only Had a Brain" when I think a head
Of straw is what this job demands. But now
The blue that's nearly trembling in the sky
Needs something flying through it.
I realize I'm whistling "White Bird"
By It's a Beautiful Day. My fiancée
And I have set the date: New Year's Eve.
The second time for both of us—I tell her
That means we've smoothed the rough spots out already.
At the last stop before the Aurora Bridge,
A man—young but clean-cut—zipped in a jacket
With lots of pockets gets on. I think no change
Will come from any of them, but he pulls out
The exact fare in quarters. He takes a seat
Across from me as we start to cross the span.

II. The Rider

I've been a fucking clerk in men's clothing
For nearly fifteen years! *Too long for lunch—*

The manager's excuse to shitcan me.
Sure, I took a little extra time to chew
The diner's stringy Reubens, more fat than meat.
I was only trying to get back a bit
Of what they've screwed me out of.
You were warned before—like my gym teacher
Back in ninth grade, suspending me
For smoking in the locker room.
What's this driver whistling for?
What the hell's *he* got to be so happy about?

III. The Teenager

I crank my Walkman up, so all I hear
Is music: the way the world's supposed to be.
Getting on the bus, I glance at the driver
Just long enough to grab my transfer. I pass
The spaced-out dirtbag in the Seahawks ball cap
And maroon sweatshirt quick as I can.
He stinks—why's the driver let him on?
From the back I see a dude in a big coat—
Cute! jawline and hair like an action hero—
Get on and sit up front. Switching tunes,
I look outside: a sky this blue seems weird
For Thanksgiving. I want snow.

IV. The Teacher

This blue reminds me of the Adriatic.
I taught the classics all my life. Finally,
Last year when I retired, I saw and walked
The lands that made them. *You're a grandmother,*
My son said: his code for *You're too old*

For travel. I told him it took twelve hours
To deliver him—pain like I was pushing out
A bowling ball. After that I can survive
Anything. On my way to his place now
To visit the grandkids, I watch a man get on;
His army jacket bulky, the color of moss.
We're heading for the Aurora Bridge, named
After the Roman goddess of the dawn.
With the sun outside, it seems the man is dressed
For another sort of weather. A graphite gleam
Like pencil lead—am I really seeing?—
As he slowly pulls something out of his pocket.

V. The Driver

It feels like my whole side's gone deaf
And numb: I can't keep the wheel from lurching
Left. I dodge the cars, they're swerving
Everywhere, I'm crushing the brakes, my leg
Stiff straight—God! my side hurts—
The stone railing bursts away, only
Blue, for a moment flying, then the bus
Dips down and the blue goes out.

VI. The Rider

Against the curb, the cars I pass
Look rooted: gawkers who've seen
Something without wings break
Into the air. A siren's growing—
I don't turn around. Why am I alive?
I thought that shot was for the manager.
Why didn't I wait? The driver.

His goddamn whistling. What gave him
The right? Why is my hand
So heavy? The gun. None of this
Makes sense. I pull on doors
Till I find an unlocked car,
Tumble in behind the wheel.
I'm burning up inside—I leave
The door open. It isn't fair:
This isn't how it should've happened.
My face is dripping—I'm burning up.
I lift the gun, staring
At its barrel. The metal ring
Of its mouth feels cool
Against the skin beneath my chin.

VII. The Police Officer

How in hell did the driver end up
On this roof? Coming down, the bus must've clipped
The corner of the apartment building. Thrown
Through the windshield. When I saw the EMTs
Haul a guy in a red sweatshirt out
Of the crumpled wreck, something told me *Check
The roof.* Been pumping the driver's chest
Since I found him. *Hang in there, pal,*
I keep on saying. His side is bleeding bad,
But I get his eyes to open—he looks at me,
Seems to know I'm here. I pump harder,
Not afraid to break a rib. *Ambulance
Is on the way,* I puff. But now his eyes
Are looking somewhere else, like he's watching
Someone over my shoulder. I turn around—

It's just us two on this roof. I push some more;
He doesn't blink. I say *Come on don't do this*
To us. My wrists will hurt for a week.

VIII. The Driver

A face forms over me. A man is leaning
On my chest—I'm lying flat beneath his hands—
Is he afraid I'll float away? He tries
To weld his eyes to mine. To make a bridge
That I can follow back with him. But the blue
I've passed through is pulsing brighter,
Darkening his face. Far overhead—
What is that? A seagull crossing the sky.
White bird   White bird must fly

IX. The Immigrant

Because of the war, I left Vietnam. Hard
To go—many relatives and friends said,
Stay; times will get better. I saw
Too many bad things: wounded people,
Bodies stiff as fallen statues. One day
I visited the village of my aunt and uncle.
The soldiers came—set fire to all of it,
No matter there were no VC. I told
My friends I was leaving then. They said, *Why go*
To America? With a tiger, the safest place
To live is behind it—in the shadow of its tail.
Came here, and found a land that knew no war
Made a game of danger: gunfire on TV
Leaves little blood. Even on the roller coaster
At Seattle Center, the screams from falling

Aren't real screams. Not like the screams that day
On the bus. I heard the gunshot—knew it was real,
And gripped the handle on the seat in front of me
Tighter than the roller coaster's. After the crash,
I at last let go. I climbed over a dead
White grandma out a shattered window.
Screams inside from a girl with purple hair
And a bleeding face were the same as back
In the war. I got to my feet, started to run—
Ran till I was out of breath. Then I looked
Back at the wreck: still too close, so I ran
Some more. Months passed, but most nights
Dreams of the crash open my eyes to dark.
So bad tonight, I'm afraid to sleep here
Any more. I called my family in Vietnam—
Tomorrow I fly back.

About the Author

Michael Spence spent a hitch as a junior naval officer aboard the aircraft carrier USS *John F. Kennedy* (CV-67), then returned to Seattle, where he spent thirty years driving public-transit buses in the Seattle area. He has three previous poetry collections: *The Spine* (Purdue University Press, 1987), *Adam Chooses* (Rose Alley Press, 1998), and *Crush Depth* (Truman State University Press, 2009). *The Bus Driver's Threnody* was a finalist for The New Criterion Poetry Prize.

In 1990, Spence was awarded a Creative Writing Fellowship from the National Endowment for the Arts, and he has received half a dozen nominations for a Pushcart Prize. His work has appeared in many magazines, including *The American Scholar*, *The Chariton Review*, *The Gettysburg Review*, *The Hopkins Review*, *The Hudson Review*, *Literary Imagination*, *Measure*, *The New Criterion*, *The New Republic*, *The North American Review*, *Poetry*, *Poetry Northwest*, *The Sewanee Review*, *The Southern Review*, *Tampa Review*, *Tar River Poetry*, and *The Yale Review*. In 2014, he was awarded a Literary Fellowship from Artist Trust of Washington State.